⦿B♥DY BITS⦿

RAISING
HUMAN
BODY
FACTS

Rotherham Schools Loan Service
Bailey House
Rawmarsh Road, Rotherham S60 1TD

This book must be returned by the date specified at the time of issue as
the DUE DATE FOR RETURN
The loan may be extended (personally, by post, telephone or online) for
a further period, if the book is not required by another reader, by quoting
the barcode / author / title.

Enquiries: 01709 822288

www.rotherham.gov.uk/sls

by **Paul Mason** and **Dave Smith**

WAYLAND
www.waylandbooks.co.uk

First published in Great Britain in 2020 by Wayland

Text and illustrations copyright © Hodder & Stoughton, 2020

All rights reserved.

Editors: Melanie Palmer and Grace Glendinning
Designer: Peter Scoulding
Illustrations: Dave Smith

ISBN: 978 1 5263 1288 4 HBK

ISBN: 978 1 5263 1289 1 PBK

An imprint of
Hachette Children's Group
Part of Hodder & Stoughton

Carmelite House
50 Victoria Embankment
London EC4Y 0DZ

An Hachette UK Company
www.hachette.co.uk
www.hachettechildrens.co.uk

Printed in China

MIX
Paper from
responsible sources
FSC® C104740
FSC
www.fsc.org

ROTHERHAM
SCHOOLS LOANS SERVICE

55 072 529 9	
CPC412700-1	J612
PETERS	£8.99

Picture credits:
Anatomical Travelogue/SPL: 20t. Bettmann/Getty Images: 26c. Olga Bolbot/
Shutterstock: 18t. DONOT6_STUDIO/Shutterstock: 21t. dpa /Alamy: 23bc. Marian
Fil/Shutterstock: 16b. Sergey Furtaev/Shutterstock: 13t. Deyan Georgiev/
Shutterstock: 20c. Jeff Gilbert/Alamy: 17 t. Pascal Goetgheluck/SPL: 8b. Steve
Gschmeissner/SPL: 12c. Imagine China/Alamy: 7 b. Eric Isselee/Shutterstock:
13b. Kalcutta/Shutterstock: 4bl. khai9000/iStock: 13c. Heinz Kluetmeier/
Sports Illustrated/Getty Images: 15b. Kues/Shutterstock: 6c. Liya Graphics/
Shutterstock: 24c. Dr John Mazziotta et al/SPL: 29b. Mediscan/Alamy: 23br.
msgrafixx/Shutterstock: 29c. Phillipp Nicolai/Shutterstock: 14t. Claudia Paulusson/
Shutterstock: 5t. Hafiez Razali/Shutterstock: 10b. Science History Images/Alamy:
23bl. Danny Smythe/Shutterstock: 19t. sruilk/Shutterstock: 22t. Videologia/
Shutterstock: 12t.

Every attempt has been made to clear copyright. Should there be any
inadvertent omission please apply to the publisher for rectification.

The website addresses (URLs) included in this book were valid at the time of
going to press. However, it is possible that contents or addresses may have
changed since the publication of this book. No responsibility for any such
changes can be accepted by either the author or the Publisher.

Contents

Body bits

Your body is made up of a LOT of different bits. While keeping you alive, your body bits do amazing, astounding, hair-raising and sometimes downright revolting things. Here are a few facts about your body that you might find surprising.

You're not totally human

Nine out of every ten cells that make up your body are not actually human. Among them are billions and billions of bacteria.

You have a LOT of body bits

You are made up of about 7 octillion atoms (written out in full, this is 7,000,000,000,000,000,000,000,000,000) and, scientists estimate, about 37 trillion cells (37,000,000,000,000).

Tiny mites* hide in the hair follicles on your skin during the day, then come out at night.

Night, night, Johnny.

I'll never sleep again.

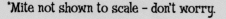

*Mite not shown to scale – don't worry.

4

You're really fast

The fastest muscles in the human body are eye muscles: they can blink in less than 0.01 of a second. Your tongue can detect a taste (for example, rotten food) even faster, in 0.0015 of a second.

You didn't start life clever

If babies had fully developed brains, their heads would be too big to be born. Right away, though, baby brains develop lots of connections called synapses. By three years old, they have about 1,000 trillion connections in place.

You get a new set of skin about every 28 days

The outside layer of your skin is constantly being rubbed off, then replaced by new skin from underneath. Most seventy-year-olds have lost about 50 kg of skin in their lifetime.

The human body is pretty hair-raising. Whether it's the fact that you are as hairy as a gorilla, or the way some people can breathe in and out at the same time, or even the reasons we get wrinkly when we're old – there are lots of freaky facts to discover in this book!

Hair-raising and nail-biting facts

Q: What do you and a rhinoceros have in common?
A: Your hair, your nails and a rhino's horn are all made of the same thing: keratin.

Hairy humans

Each hair on your body grows out of a follicle in your skin. Humans have about 5 million hair follicles, which is almost exactly the same as a gorilla has. Most human hairs are just a lot harder to see than a gorilla's.

The only parts of human skin that aren't hairy are the soles of your feet, the palms of your hands and your lips.

Honestly! Just look a bit closer.

SCIENCE FLASH

Your hair is dead, except at the place where it grows from your body. Because it was originally connected to your blood supply, your hair contains a record of things that travelled through your blood while it was growing. Scientists can analyse hair to find out, for example, what food people ate even months before.

strong hair

A strand of human hair can support up to 100 g. That might not sound like much, but you have an average of 100,000–150,000 strands on your head. If all your hair could be woven into a thick rope, it would be strong enough to hold up two elephants.

Seasonal nails

Your nails are constantly growing (on average, 3–4 mm a month), but they don't all grow at the same speed. Fingernails grow faster than toenails, though the little fingernail is the slowest on your hand. All nails grow faster in sunlight, and so grow more speedily in summer.

SCIENCE FLASH

Your fingernails help make your fingertips more sensitive. When you press down on something, your hard fingernails resist. Your brain works out how much more you have to press to feel pressure on your fingertips as well. This tells your brain how soft or hard the object is.

Excellent eyeballs

Your eyes are the second-most complex organ in your body, after your brain. Each eyeball has more than 2 million moving parts.

The earliest humans all had brown eyes. Blue eyes first appeared about 6,000 years ago.

The radical retina

At the back of your eye is a thin layer of cells called the retina. This is where light gets turned into signals your brain can understand. Every person's retina is unique – far more unique than fingerprints. Even identical twins have different blood vessel patterns in their retina.

When people's eyes look red in a photo, it's because the blood vessels inside are being lit up.

SCIENCE FLASH

The cornea – that clear layer over the front of the eye – is the only living part of the body without a blood supply. It doesn't have one because you wouldn't be able to see through blood vessels. The cornea gets its oxygen from air.

You can only see about 1/6th of a person's eyeball. The rest is kept safe inside its socket.

Eyelashes

Eyelashes keep dirt and dust out of your eyes. They also trigger them to shut if something comes too close. Each eyelash lasts 3–5 months, then falls out: a lifetime's eyelashes laid end-to-end would stretch about 3 m.

Everyone has tiny mites living in their eyelash follicles. It is not known whether the mites move house before their eyelash 'home' falls out.

Do we really have to move **AGAIN**?

A good cry

Tear ducts in the corners of your eyes release fluid. It helps your eyes move easily when you look around. Every time you blink, the fluid washes your eyeball, a bit like a car windscreen squirter. Human tear ducts also leak fluid when we are upset. Experts think that humans are the only animals to cry like this.

I just wanted a little snack ...

Crocodiles don't cry when they are upset – they cry when they bite into something. Their eyes seem to leak as they eat. 'Crocodile tears' aren't to trick people; they're just biology!

9

The boggling brain

Human brains really are mind-boggling. They do most of their jobs without having to be told. You don't, for example, need to think, "Breathe in, lungs," or, "Heart, keep beating."

What are brains made of?

Mostly fat. Not the bit that does the thinking, but still, your brain is about 60 per cent fat. The thinking bits are neuron cells, connected by synapses. The brain contains about 100 billion neurons.

Depending on the situation, the brain can respond in as little as 1/10,000th of a second.

I've got it from here.

Brains never sleep

Your brain is actually busier when you're asleep than when you're awake. It needs sleep to work properly. Without enough sleep, it starts to lose its ability to create memories.

SCIENCE FLASH

There are lots of myths about the brain – but are any of them true?

MYTH 1: You only use 10 per cent of your brain.	False: We use much more of our brains than this – just not all at the same time.
MYTH 2: Brain size determines intelligence.	False: When the brain of genius scientist Albert Einstein was examined, it was average weight. However, the number of connections, or synapses, in his brain was above-average.
MYTH 3: People are left-brained or right-brained.	False: It was once thought that either the left or right side of people's brains was dominant, affecting their skills and behaviour. There is no evidence to support this as the reason for our differences.
MYTH 4: Your brain shrinks as you get older.	True: But it's only little by little after you're forty years old, and not in any great amount until after you're seventy, on average.
MYTH 5: Ice cream gives you a headache.	True: When your brain senses a sudden drop in temperature on your tongue, it increases blood pressure FAST. This makes your head hurt for a few moments.

Brains don't feel pain

Our brains have no pain receptors. This means brain surgeons can operate on someone's brain while they are awake!

CHEESE!

The truth about teeth

Teeth *look* like bone, they're white like bone, and they're hard like bone – but they're not bone. They're actually like nothing else in your body.

Tough teeth

Teeth are harder on the outside than even the hardest bone in your body (your jawbone). This outer layer, the enamel, can resist thousands of kilograms of squashing force. New research has shown that enamel is formed in a criss-cross structure. If a crack does start to form, this structure stops it spreading.

Enamel under a microscope

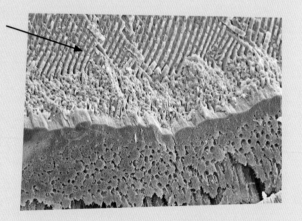

Baby teeth

Human teeth start to form well before birth. At this stage they are buried inside our gums. Teeth usually begin to stick through the gums when we're a few months old, but for some it happens sooner: the record for 'most teeth at birth' is TWELVE!

SCIENCE FLASH

The enamel exterior of a human tooth is rated 5 on the Mohs hardness scale of 1–10. That makes teeth harder than iron or steel.

YEUW!

Bacteria live in everyone's mouth. These tiny creatures release acids that eat away at your teeth. The only way to stop your teeth rotting is to clean away the bacteria.

NOM

NOM NOM

Squirt

In medieval Germany, some people thought toothache could be cured by kissing a donkey.

Some early toothbrush heads were made of boar bristles.

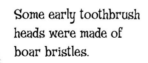

No you may **NOT** rub your teeth on me!

Cleaning teeth

If you ever think cleaning your teeth is a pain, remember: it could be worse. The first known tooth-cleaning tools date from about 5,500 years ago. They were sticks of wood with frayed ends. The wood contains natural chemicals that fight bacteria. In fact, some people around the world still use this method to clean their teeth today.

In ancient Greece and Rome, people used ashes, or ground-up oyster shells, bones and hoofs, as toothpaste.

13

Brilliant bones

Without bones, you couldn't stand up. In fact, your skeleton is what makes you human-shaped, instead of puddle-on-the-floor-shaped.

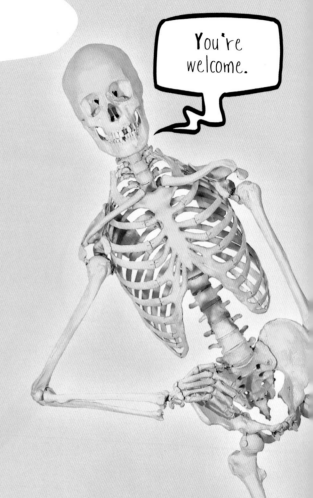

You're welcome.

Baby bones

Human babies start life with about 300 bones. As they grow, some join together. Most adults end up with 206 bones, though some people have two extra or two fewer ribs.

One bone babies *don't* have is a kneecap. Instead they have a bit of tough, spongy material in front of their knee joints. By the time they're about four years old and have stopped falling over all the time, this spongy material starts to turn into bone.

I can't wait till I have kneecaps!

Backbones

Your backbone (or spine) is actually made up of thirty-three separate bones. They're linked by dozens of muscles, over 200 tough ligaments and some squishy cartilage.

When you're standing up, gravity squishes your spine's cartilage. This makes most people a tiny bit shorter by the time they go to bed. Over the age of about forty-five, people start to shrink permanently from all the squishing!

other jobs for bones

As well as supporting your body, bones have other jobs:

• Without the hyoid bone in your throat, you wouldn't be able to speak. This bone also acts as an anchor for your tongue, allowing it a wide range of movement.

• Your ribs protect your vital organs from damage.

• Bones help you recover from illness, because virus-killing cells (lymphocytes) are manufactured in your bone marrow.

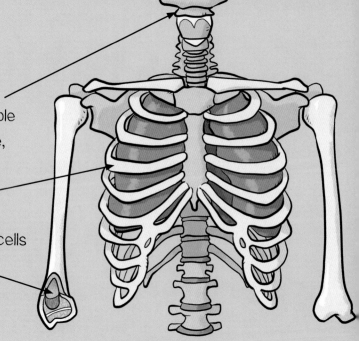

Bone repair

When bones break, they repair themselves amazingly well. It takes 6–12 weeks, depending on what is broken and how old you are. Children usually heal much faster than adults.

Record-breaking stunt rider Evel Knievel fractured bones 433 times during his career (quite an achievement, considering he only had 206 to break).

Here he goes again ...

Breathtaking breathing

Did you know that most people breathe mainly through just one nostril at a time? Their body usually changes which one it's using every few hours.

Large lungs

The air you breathe in ends up in your lungs, which contain over 2,000 km of airways. Unravelled, they would stretch almost halfway across the United States. You breathe in about 8,500 litres of air every day. In your lifetime, you'll probably breathe in enough air (250 million litres) to fill a hundred Olympic-sized pools.

I need some breathing room!

Your lungs are different sizes and shapes. Your right one is wider and has three parts. The left is thinner and has two (it has to squish up a bit to make room for your heart).

Push OVER!

Yawning

Experts think we yawn to breathe in lots of oxygen quickly, when our bodies need an extra boost. This is why people yawn most often if they are tired or scared. When you are scared, your body thinks it might have to fight or run away – so it calls for extra oxygen.

Freaky breathers

Not everyone always breathes in, out, in, out, etc. Musicians who play didgeridoo, zuma and some other wind instruments can do 'circular breathing'. They breathe in through their nose and out through their mouth at the same time.

In 2017, the Nigerian saxophone player Femi Kuti used circular breathing to play a continuous note for 51 minutes, 35 seconds.

Does he know any other notes?

SCIENCE FLASH

Hiccups happen when a sheet of muscle called the diaphragm, which usually helps you breathe, gets irritated and does a sudden jerky movement. This pulls air quickly into the lungs, which causes a little 'hic!' Hiccups usually go away in a few minutes, which is a good job – there is no guaranteed cure for them.

HiCCUP!

Bits about blood

Blood is one of the most amazing parts of the human body. For example, did you know that blood contains tiny traces of gold?

Blood facts

The human body naturally contains about 0.2 mg of gold, and most of it is in our blood. In fact, there are many metals in blood, such as cobalt and iron, which are essential to blood health. But blood is *mostly* made up of red blood cells, white blood cells and platelets, held in a liquid called plasma.

SCIENCE FLASH

When air is sucked down into your lungs, oxygen is removed and added to your blood, which then travels to your heart. Oxygen-rich blood is pumped by the heart around the rest of your body.

Ted!

Hey, Frank!

Thanks a clot!

· Red blood cells are transporters, carrying oxygen away from the lungs and carbon dioxide back to them.

· White blood cells fight diseases.

· Platelets help blood to clot.

Blood vessels

Blood moves around inside blood vessels. As it is pumped away from your heart, blood is under a lot of pressure. Even the tiniest hole in a blood vessel can be disastrous. Blood squirts out with each heartbeat. In seconds, there is an extreme amount of blood lost.

The biggest blood vessel is the aorta, which in an adult is a similar diameter to a garden hose.

Where does blood go?

Everywhere! Blood carries oxygen all over your body (except your cornea). If the oxygen starts to run low, there's a priority list for which bits of you get oxygen first – a bit like a mobile phone going into low-power mode. At the front of the oxygen queue is your brain.

Different bits of you need blood at different times:

After you've eaten and are digesting food, your intestines need blood.

When you're asleep, more blood goes to your brain and muscles.

While you exercise, extra blood flows to your muscles.

Stupendous skin

Your skin is the largest organ in your body. It is brilliant at its biggest job, which is keeping your insides in and the outside out. But it does a lot of other amazing things too.

SCIENCE FLASH

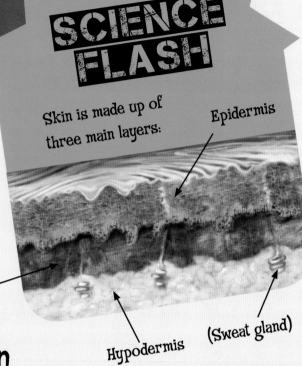

Skin is made up of three main layers:

Epidermis

Dermis

Hypodermis

(Sweat gland)

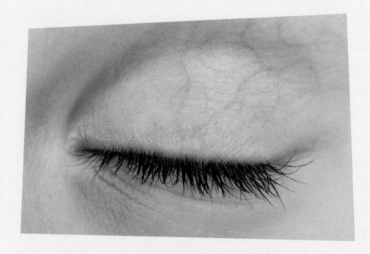

Super skin

Your skin protects your insides, keeps out diseases, lets your body feel temperature, keeps you cool and stores energy in the form of fat. Skin is thickest on your feet and thinnest on your eyelids and behind your ears.

New skin for old

Most of the 'dust' in your house is actually old skin cells. Dead cells from the outer layer are constantly coming off (becoming dust), then being replaced with new ones. As a result of all this, you get a whole new epidermis about once a month.

Why we get wrinkly

Skin gets its firmness from something called collagen. Once you are about twenty-five years old, your skin produces less collagen each year. This is not the biggest reason for wrinkles, though. Other influences such as being in the sun a lot and smoking wrinkle your skin too.

If I can just ... get ... the angle ... right ...

What's in a spot?

Everyone gets a spot once in a while. But what actually IS a spot?

A pore is a little hole in your skin that releases an oil called sebum, which stops your skin drying out. Spots happen when a pore gets blocked. Your body sends extra blood to the blockage to clear it out, which is why spots go red and inflamed.

Humans going through puberty get more spots than most people, because their skin releases more oily fluid as their hormone levels change.

Dynamic defences

Your body is great at stopping diseases and infections getting in. It's also got a well-trained defensive team for dealing with any invaders that get through.

First line of defence

As well as skin, your body is defended by hairs. The hairs in your nostrils, for example, are a barrier to dust, pollen and other bits you don't want to breathe into your lungs.

The outsides of your delicate organs are protected by mucous membranes. These are barrier layers of cells, which sometimes secrete a gloopy fluid called mucous.

Inner defences

Once in a while, something gets past your outer defences. That's when your inner defences spring into action. The most important defenders are your white blood cells, and they come in various shapes and sizes. Here are two important types:

1 Lymphocytes are part of the immune system. They remember invaders such as viruses, and destroy them if they return.

2 A phagocytic white blood cell (the green blob above) chews up invaders. Each phagocyte is a specialist, with receptors for detecting a particular kind of invader cell.

Made it! Hang on, what's this?

I'd prefer not to, if you don't ... Oh.

Well this is awkward.

It's gone all dark.

GURGLE

GURGLE

Haven't we met?

Burp!

Surprising intruders

Sometimes, intruders get into a human body by accident and are too big or awkward for the blood cells to attack. This means your digestive system – or even a doctor – has to come to the rescue. Real-life examples include:

- surgical tools that were accidentally left behind, including clamps, sponges and gloves

- food such as peas, beans or seeds stuck in earholes or sinuses

- swallowed items, including part of a fidget spinner, a lighter (which stayed inside for seventeen months), false teeth swallowed by someone who was asleep (inside them for eight days) and a pen that the patient claimed to have swallowed twenty-five years before.

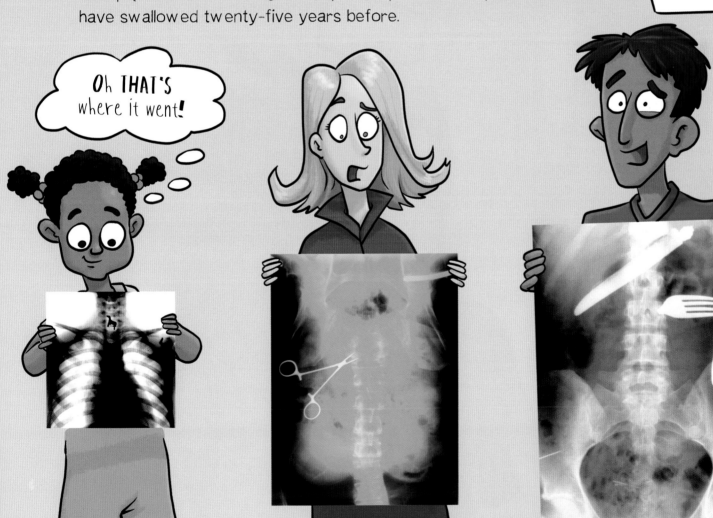

23

stomach-churning digestion

People in wealthy countries eat about 30 tonnes of food in their lifetime. This includes an average of eleven cows, thirty sheep, twenty-seven pigs, over TWO THOUSAND chickens and A LOT of fruit and veg. It all passes through their digestive system.

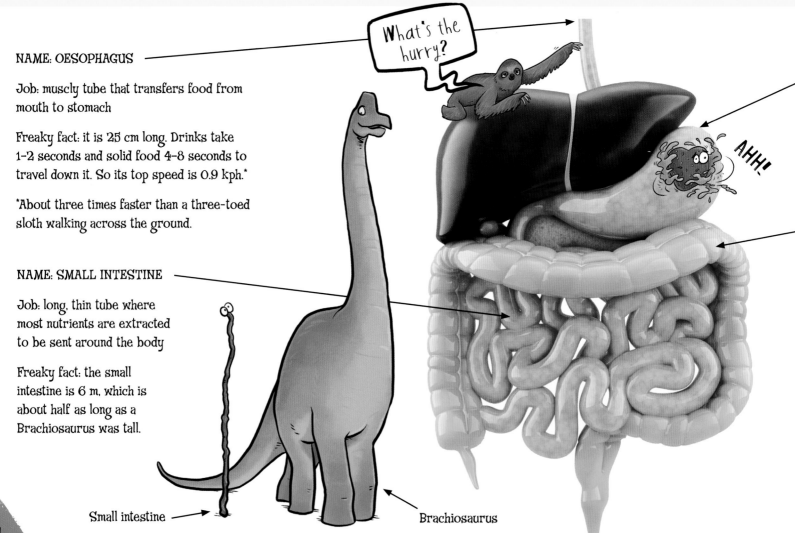

NAME: OESOPHAGUS

Job: muscly tube that transfers food from mouth to stomach

Freaky fact: it is 25 cm long. Drinks take 1-2 seconds and solid food 4-8 seconds to travel down it. So its top speed is 0.9 kph.*

*About three times faster than a three-toed sloth walking across the ground.

NAME: SMALL INTESTINE

Job: long, thin tube where most nutrients are extracted to be sent around the body

Freaky fact: the small intestine is 6 m, which is about half as long as a Brachiosaurus was tall.

What's the hurry?

AHH!

Small intestine

Brachiosaurus

Fart facts

Millions of bacteria live in your gut, helping you digest food. The by-product of this process is gaseous and can have a very eggy smell, which escapes as you fart. Everyone's gut produces this gas, whatever they tell you.

On average, healthy humans fart more than twelve times per day. People fart more if they chew gum, suck on pen tops, smoke or wear loose false teeth, all of which cause excessive air-swallowing that adds to the natural fart gases.

PFFRRT

NAME: STOMACH

Job: organ that turns food into sloppy chyme, using a combination of churning and acid.

Freaky fact: the acid means your stomach has to renew its lining every few days.

NAME: LARGE INTESTINE

Job: shorter, wider tube that removes water and final nutrients from food

Freaky fact: the large intestine is only a quarter as long as the small one. (It's still about as tall as you are, though.)

Large intestine

SCIENCE FLASH

Your gut 'talks' to your brain. Scientists have known for years that it can release 'time-to-eat' chemicals into your blood. Ten minutes later, the chemicals reach your brain and you feel hungry.

Scientists have recently discovered a super-fast link between your gut and your brain. The gut probably uses it to tell the brain you've eaten something dangerous.

Amazing muscles

Imagine a little baby ... now imagine a thirty-year-old bodybuilder. Incredibly, they have the same number of muscles.

You already have all your muscles

The muscles bodybuilders work on are called skeletal muscles (because they attach to your skeleton). Humans are born with all the skeletal muscle fibres they're ever going to have, so you can't grow new ones. What you CAN do is make them bigger. The harder and more you use them (for example, by picking up incredibly heavy weights lots of times), the more these skeletal muscles grow.

The heaviest weight lifted by a human is thought to be 2,844 kg. That's heavier than an adult rhinoceros! (The lifter, an American called Paul Anderson who is pictured above, also used to pick up tables with eight people sitting on top to show how strong he was.)

The muscle you can't live without

Your heart is your most important muscle. It is made of cardiac muscle and contracts about once a second to pump blood around your body.* Without the oxygen blood brings, your body stops working. On average, a person's heart beats about 3.3 billion times in their lifetime and pumps more than 1 million barrels of blood.

*Your pulse gets slower as you get older. Newborn babies' hearts beat about 130 times a minute. Once they are grown, this slows to 60-75 beats per minute.

Hurry up, Grandad!

SCIENCE FLASH

Human hearts have their own electrical system, which means they can carry on beating even without a body. All they need is a blood supply with proper oxygen and surroundings that will allow their cells to stay alive.

Smooth muscle

Our bodies have a third kind of muscle, called smooth muscle. Most people never think about this, because they don't have to. Smooth muscles work automatically, controlling the movements of your stomach, gut, lungs, blood vessels and more. There are even smooth muscles in your eyes, helping adjust the amount of light your pupils let in.

It's all groovy, baby.

Unique you

Most people know that we all have different fingerprints (the pattern of ridges at the end of each finger and thumb). But we have some other body bits that are unique, too.

Tongue-prints

Human tongues have a ridge down the middle and are covered in tiny bumps called papillae. These features are slightly different on everyone, in the same way as fingerprints. The size and shape of tongues are also different. Altogether they add up to a unique tongue-print.

SCIENCE FLASH

Computers can now identify people by the way they walk or run. How we move is affected by our bones, muscles and sense of balance. Computers can 'watch' a video of a walker, note the differences in their gait, and identify them in as few as four steps!

I'm afraid we'll have to tongue-print you.

Bottom

Our bottoms are all a slightly different shape. Using this fact, Japanese experts have developed a special pad with 360 sensors, which measure the shape and size of the bottom sitting on it. In theory the pad could be used to stop someone stealing your car, or sitting at your desk and using your computer.

Ears

Human ears are also all shaped differently, and ear-prints have been used to investigate crime scenes since at least the 1950s.

Ears also never stop growing: the older you get, the bigger your ears will be.

Smell

Your body is constantly giving off a fog of chemicals called a 'thermal plume'. Exactly what's in this thermal plume is different for each of us. This is why tracker dogs can follow individual scent trails.

Your brain even works differently

Even your brain is different from everyone else's. As we grow, our brains develop connections that help us do things more easily. These connections are called neural pathways. Everyone's neural pathways are different. When two people do the exact same job – picking up a ball, for example – different pathways light up in their brains.

Three different brains listening to the same piece of music.

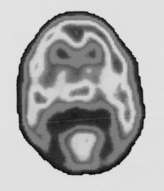
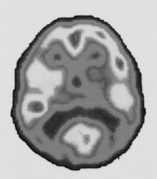
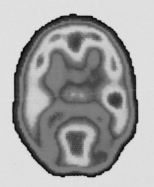

29

Glossary

atom the basic parts or units of matter

blood vessel tube that blood flows through

bristles thick, tough hairs, which usually come from a pig, boar or similar animal

carbon dioxide gas produced when humans breathe: we breathe oxygen in and carbon dioxide out

cartilage tough material found at the ends of bones and in ears, noses and other body parts

chyme churned-up liquid food in the stomach

clot blood that has become harder and stuck together

contract squeeze together or get smaller

diameter width of the widest part of a circle

diaphragm sheet of muscle below the lungs, which helps them breathe in and out

didgeridoo long tube, usually made of wood, played by blowing down it – a traditional instrument of Aboriginal Australians

dominant in charge or most powerful

follicle very small hole in the skin out of which a hair grows

gait the way a person walks

gum soft, fleshy part of your mouth that teeth grow out of

gut part of the digestive system made up of the small and large intestines

hormones chemicals made in the body that act as messengers to cells and organs around the body

immune system organs and processes that stop you getting ill, or make you better if you do catch an illness

keratin material that makes up the biggest part of body parts such as hair, horns, nails, hoofs and feathers

ligament tough, stretchy material that links bones

Mohs hardness scale measurement of how hard something is, ranging from 1 (not very hard) to 10 (very hard indeed)

nutrient something that a living thing needs to grow and/or survive

optic nerve group of nerves that carry messages from your eyes to your brain

organ individual part of a living thing that has a particular job or jobs to do (e.g. your heart, which pumps blood)

oxygen gas that humans need to breathe in to survive. Oxygen makes up about 20 per cent of air

pollen powdery substance that plants release. When pollen from one plant reaches another, the second plant can reproduce

pore tiny opening in skin. Although pores are tiny, gas, liquid and other substances can pass through them

puberty the time when a young person's body begins to grow and change into an adult body

pulse heartbeat

sebum oily liquid (or sometimes a wax) released by the skin. Sebum helps keep skin and hairs moist and waterproof

secrete slowly release a fluid

skeleton bones that together make up the supporting structure for a body

stunt rider motorcyclist, cyclist or horse rider who performs tricks and daredevil acts

zuma horn-like wind instrument played in eastern Europe, western Asia and north Africa

Finding out more

Books to read

For more information about how the human body works, the 'Bright and Bold Human Body' series is a great place to start. All published in 2020 by Wayland, there are books on *The Digestive System*, *The Heart*, *Lungs and Blood*, *The Brain and Nervous System*, *The Reproductive System*, *The Skeleton and Muscles*, and *The Senses*.

If you'd like an overview of the most important facts about the human body all in one book, the colourful and engaging *100 Questions About The Human Body* by Simon Abbott (Peter Pauper Press, 2019) is a good place to look.

What happens when things don't go according to plan for the human body? To investigate, hustle down to the library and find yourself a copy of *Cause, Effect and Chaos in the Human Body* by Paul Mason (Wayland, 2020).

For more freaky facts about the human body, you could try:

A Question of Science: Human Body
By Anna Claybourne (Wayland, 2020)

Human Body: A Monster Activity Book, which contains some fun experiments and press-out models
(Igloo Books, 2019)

Boom Science: Human Body
By Georgia Amson-Bradshaw (PowerKids Press, 2019)

Places to visit

In London, some of the best places to visit to find out about the human body are:

Not for the faint-hearted, but still fascinating, is Bodyworlds, (London Pavilion, 1 Piccadilly Circus, London W1J 0DA). The museum features real-life human bodies preserved for educational purposes (with the permission of their original owners).

The Science Museum (Exhibition Road, South Kensington, London SW7 2DD), especially the 'Who Am I?' and 'Medicine' collections.
Website: sciencemuseum.org.uk

Round the corner from the Science Museum is the Natural History Museum (Cromwell Road, London SW7 5BD), which has a good Human Biology gallery.

Other great human-body and anatomy museums in the UK include:

The Hunterian in Glasgow (gla.ac.uk/hunterian, visits by appointment)

The Anatomy Museum at the University of Edinburgh (ed.ac.uk/biomedical-sciences/anatomy/anatomical-museum, open on select days).

Index

The book is OVER?!